Much Love, Cody Goglan ♡ "Twinkle"

TO Charlie Maddison
FROM Grandma
DATE March 20, 2018

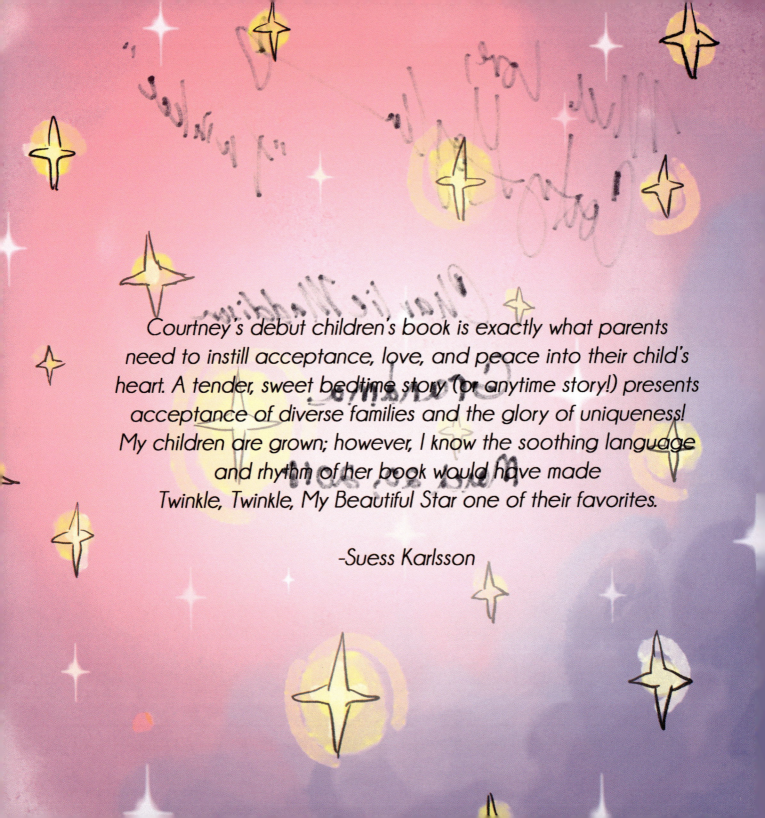

Courtney's debut children's book is exactly what parents need to instill acceptance, love, and peace into their child's heart. A tender, sweet bedtime story (or anytime story!) presents acceptance of diverse families and the glory of uniqueness! My children are grown; however, I know the soothing language and rhythm of her book would have made Twinkle, Twinkle, My Beautiful Star one of their favorites.

-Suess Karlsson

Twinkle, Twinkle, My Beautiful Star

COURTNEY K. GOGLIORMELLA

ILLUSTRATED BY MYKYTA HARETS

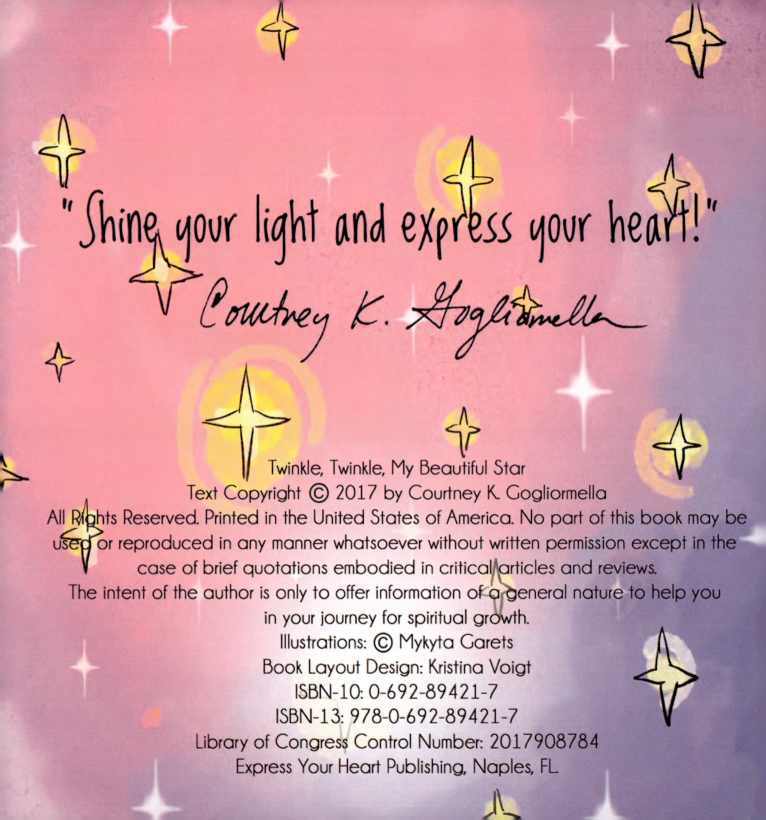

"Shine your light and express your heart!"

Courtney K. Gogliormella

Twinkle, Twinkle, My Beautiful Star
Text Copyright © 2017 by Courtney K. Gogliormella
All Rights Reserved. Printed in the United States of America. No part of this book may be used or reproduced in any manner whatsoever without written permission except in the case of brief quotations embodied in critical articles and reviews.
The intent of the author is only to offer information of a general nature to help you in your journey for spiritual growth.
Illustrations: © Mykyta Garets
Book Layout Design: Kristina Voigt
ISBN-10: 0-692-89421-7
ISBN-13: 978-0-692-89421-7
Library of Congress Control Number: 2017908784
Express Your Heart Publishing, Naples, FL.

To My Readers

Dear Beautiful Spirits,

I'm so grateful you have purchased Twinkle, Twinkle, My Beautiful Star. This book is an expression of love and acceptance for all children and adults! I wrote this book to bring children and their families the gift of love and acceptance. I share with you, that the children's Creator loves them for exactly who they are, and it doesn't matter what family they came into the world with. We are all equal and loved by our Creator! (whomever that may be) All children get to know they twinkle and are beautiful lights in the world. Children get to live and be who they are. . . . most importantly, they should be themselves. Children are beautiful spirits and should shine their beautiful lights. In this book, they have the opportunity to see different types of families and know each one is unique and perfect. As adults, it is our responsibility to love and show our full acceptance to our children, exactly as their Creator does. Our Creator makes no mistakes and loves each child and adult completely!

Dreams do come true,

Courtney K. Hogliomella

Beautiful Child,

Twinkle, Twinkle, My Beautiful Star. I love you just the way you are! No matter who you are or where you come from, you are whole and complete. I made you. I love you so much!!!

Twinkle, Sparkle, and Shine,

Your Creator

Paint, Paint, my beautiful star-
Below the sky so wide!
I KNOW exactly who you are,
I love you, at all times!

I am in you- you are in Me!
I am all around!
I am the earth and the sky.
I am the sun,
the moon and the stars at night.
I am the air that you breathe and the breeze that moves the leaves in the trees!

I dedicate and give thanks to my Creator whom I choose to call God for inspiring me to write this book. Thank you to the many people along my journey who believe in me and encourage me to follow my dreams. In deepest appreciation: Sharon Gogliormella (my Mom), Kristina Voigt (Sister and Book Layout Designer), Riley, Chase and Tony Voigt, Suess Karlsson (dear friend, Mentor and Editor), Samantha Duffy (Photographer), Mykyta Harets (Illustrator and Cover Design), Patti Jans (Guest Editor), Tiffany Witt, Ally Seider, Neil Benecke Jr., Andrea Clair, Peter Goggin, Gramps and Debbie Jorgensen, Auntie Kathy Evans, Auntie Judy and Uncle John McCabe, Janet Jorgensen, Nono and Noni Gogliormella, Michael Gogliormella, Karen Eldred, Cynthia Davis, Sarah Brown, Katie Hope, Alyson Ellwel, Joanna Fedrowitz, Haley Dutchka and Grace Dutchka, Stacey, Andrea and Hadley Huber Balogh, Christine Arigo, Lindsey, Rob and Brayden Finnie, Bob Munn, Kay, Michael, Kaleah and Carter Smith, Jesus Rodriguez, Brian Tassinari, Kyle Banta, Melody Rogers, Cass Wyant, Betty Norqual, Ashley Davene, Angela A. Chapko, Jennette Gluski, Ralph Gogliormella, Matt Dedio, DeAnna Graziano, Auntie Theresa Lorenzo, Leela, Buddie, Anna, Cooper, and my many other friends and family. You know who you are!
Thank you! Thank you! Thank you!
I am overflowing in joy and appreciation!

Courtney Kathleen Gogliormella loves life and people! Courtney's dream has come true with this book. She lives her purpose which she believes is to bring love and acceptance into the world. She is a beaming light of appreciation and smiles to all that know her! Courtney understands first-hand what it feels like when others choose to not love and accept her for who she is. Her gift is to show the world that there is a Creator (whoever that is for you) that loves and accepts you just the way you are. She has lived in Naples, Florida most of her life but is originally from Boston, Massachusetts. Courtney is a Certified Dental Assistant, Entrepreneur, Inspirational Speaker, Artist, Empath, Lightworker, Indigo Child and Adult, and now an Author.

Mykyta Harets, also know as Nikita Harets, is a Ukrainian illustrator, born 1989. He graduated from the Dnipropetrovsk Music College (cello class) and Dnipropetrovsk College of Theatre and Arts. After having started his professional career in music, he turned to fine arts and theatre. He has been working in his own NATIVE style for the last three years; designing only the most interesting and exciting books. He carries out personal exhibitions as an independent artist participating in international fairs and festivals. His main goal is to display the story of books through the prism of his artistic perception, while maintaining childlike spontaneity and simplicity.